anythink

NO LONGER PROPERTY OF
ANYTHINK LIBRARIES/
RANGEVIEW LIBRARY DISTRICT

DISCOVER EARTH SCIENCE

ALL ABOUT EARTH

Exploring the Planet with SCIENCE PROJECTS

by Sara L. Latta

Consultant:
Daniel S. Jones, Research Associate
Department of Earth Sciences & BioTechnology Institute
University of Minnesota

CAPSTONE PRESS
a capstone imprint

Fact Finders Books are published by Capstone Press,
1710 Roe Crest Drive, North Mankato, Minnesota 56003
www.capstonepub.com

Copyright © 2016 by Capstone Press, a Capstone imprint. All rights reserved.
No part of this publication may be reproduced in whole or in part, or stored in a
retrieval system, or transmitted in any form or by any means, electronic, mechanical,
photocopying, recording, or otherwise, without written permission of the publisher.

Library of Congress Cataloging-in-Publication Data
Latta, Sara L., author.
 All about Earth : exploring the planet with science projects / by Sara L. Latta.
    pages cm.—(Fact finders. Discover earth science)
 Summary: "Step-by-step instructions for activities pertaining to Earth,
including its rotation in space, seasons, gravity, and matter"—Provided by publisher.
 Includes bibliographical references and index.
 ISBN 978-1-4914-4814-4 (library binding)
 ISBN 978-1-4914-4913-4 (eBook PDF)
1. Earth sciences—Experiments—Juvenile literature. 2. Earth sciences—Juvenile
literature. 3. Science projects—Juvenile literature. I. Title.
 QE29.L38 2016
 550.78—dc23   2014048011

Editorial Credits
Alesha Sullivan, editor; Sarah Bennett, designer; Kelly Garvin, media researcher;
Lori Barbeau, production specialist

Photo Credits
Capstone Press/Karon Dubke, 8, 12, 13, 16, 19, 21, 22, 26 (right), 27 (left), 29;
Shutterstock: Dennis van de Water, 10-11, Designua, 9 (inset map), Everett Historical,
27 (bottom right), Hluboki Dzianis, 27 (right), Jelena Ž, 28, microvector, 24,
monticello, 17, Nikitina Olga, 18, Olga_Phoenix, 20-21, Pavelk, 14, Sarah Barry, cover,
serhio, 26 (left), Tamara Kulikova, 6-7, tentor, 28 (bottom), Thitisan, 15, 25, Triff, 4-5,
UbjsP, 11 (top right), Willyam Bradberry, 9, v777999, 22-23

Design Elements: Shutterstock: Curly Pat, Magnia, Markovka, Ms.Moloko, Orfeev,
pockygallery, Sashatigar, yingphoto

Printed in the United States of America in Stevens Point, Wisconsin.
032015   008824WZF15

Table of Contents

The Science in and around the Planet

Imagine flying in space and looking down at Earth. You might think it looks like a big glass marble swirled with blue, white, green, and brown. It's the only planet we know of that can support living things, from ants to elephants—and you.

Did you know that life on Earth could not exist without the sun? And that many forms of life on Earth revolve around various cycles? Without the water cycle, for example, the weather outside would never change. Learn about some of Earth's systems through simple experiments that you can do in your own home and backyard!

You can do most of the projects on your own or with the help of a friend. But some of these experiments may require an adult's help. Think safety first! And remember, science can sometimes be messy—so don't forget to clean up when you're done. Now roll up your sleeves, grab a notebook, and dig in!

Create Convection Currents

Is it windy outside? That's because **convection** currents are at work! Convection currents play a big role in Earth's **climate**. Currents in the air and oceans move **energy** in the form of heat from one part of the globe to another. This happens constantly in the ocean when cold water mixes with warm water near the **equator**.

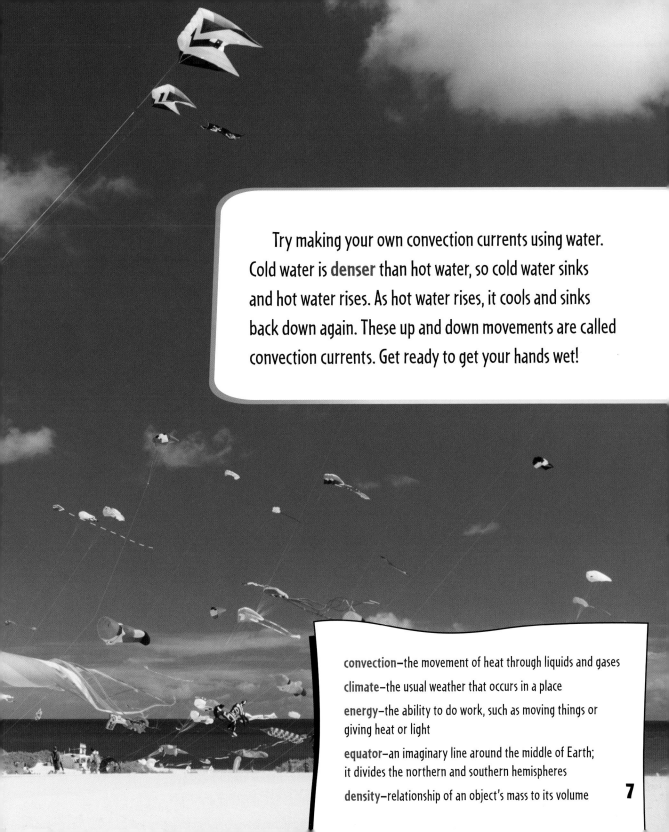

Try making your own convection currents using water. Cold water is **denser** than hot water, so cold water sinks and hot water rises. As hot water rises, it cools and sinks back down again. These up and down movements are called convection currents. Get ready to get your hands wet!

convection—the movement of heat through liquids and gases

climate—the usual weather that occurs in a place

energy—the ability to do work, such as moving things or giving heat or light

equator—an imaginary line around the middle of Earth; it divides the northern and southern hemispheres

density—relationship of an object's mass to its volume

What You Do

What You Need

bowl

blue and red food coloring

water

ice cube tray

clear plastic container

drinking glass

1. In a bowl, add blue food coloring to water, and pour the water into an ice cube tray.

2. Place in a freezer for a couple of hours or until frozen.

3. After the cubes are frozen, fill a clear plastic container two-thirds full of room **temperature** water. Wait for the water to become completely still.

4. Warm a bottle of red food coloring by setting it in a glass of hot water.

5. Next place a blue ice cube in the room temperature water in the plastic container. Place the ice cube in the middle of the container.

6. Put two drops of warm red food coloring in the plastic container of water with the blue ice cube. Drop the food coloring into the side of the container, away from the ice cube.

7. Try not to disturb the water.

Observe where the warm red water moves. Where does the cold blue ice cube move? Which color sinks? Which one rises?

temperature—the measure of how hot or cold something is; room temperature is typically a comfortable 70 degrees Fahrenheit (21 degrees Celsius)

How Does the Ocean Affect Climate?

Convection currents cycle water and air from the warm equator to the cold North and South Poles and then back again. Scientists call this the "great ocean conveyor belt."

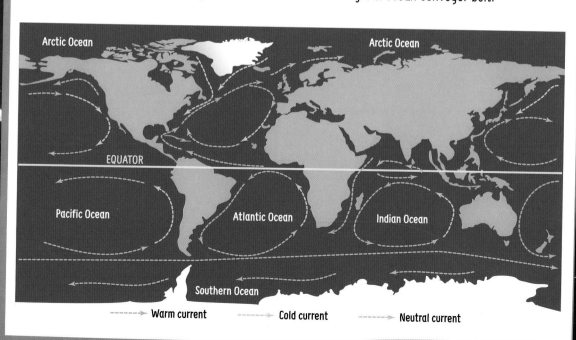

Arctic Ocean

Arctic Ocean

EQUATOR

Pacific Ocean

Atlantic Ocean

Indian Ocean

Southern Ocean

- - - -▷ Warm current   - - - -▷ Cold current   - - - -▷ Neutral current

Become a Weather Reporter

Weather is all around us. Is it hot or cold outside? Is it rainy or snowy? Is it windy or calm? Wind is especially important for some jobs and in nature. It's more difficult to fly an airplane when there are high winds, for example. It may also be difficult for plants to grow in a windy spot.

Wind speed is the movement of air from **high pressure** to **low pressure**. You can make an instrument called an **anemometer** to measure wind speed—just like the weather forecasters on TV or the radio!

FACT

Scientists use anemometers to help them forecast storms and changes in weather patterns.

high pressure–a condition of the atmosphere in which the pressure is above average

low pressure–a condition of the atmosphere in which the pressure is below average

anemometer–a scientific instrument used to measure wind speed

What You Do

1. Slide the end of one straw inside the end of another. Repeat with the other two straws. You will have two long straws.

What You Need

4 straight plastic drinking straws

straight pin

pencil with eraser

tape

stapler

4 small paper cups (3 of the same color and 1 of a different color)

stopwatch, timer, or watch with a second hand

2. Arrange the joined drinking straws to form an "X." Push a straight pin through the straws at the center of the "X" and anchor it into the eraser. If the pin doesn't hold the "X" well enough, use a bit of tape to secure.

3. Staple the top side of a cup to one of the straw ends. Repeat this for the other three cups. Make sure that the open ends of the cups face upward. Blow on the cups to make sure they spin easily. Now you're ready to measure wind speed!

Helpful Hint: To make it spin easier, you may need to wiggle the straws around the pinhole to widen the hole a bit.

4. Take your anemometer outside when the wind is blowing. If it isn't windy, stand in front of a fan indoors.

5. Ask a friend to use a stopwatch to time 60 seconds. Count how many times the colored cup completes a full circle. This is the number of rotations per minute.

Ten turns per minute of your anemometer means that the wind speed is about 1 mile (1.6 kilometers) per hour. How fast is the wind speed where you live? Report your findings to your family and friends!

Build Your Own Greenhouse

On Earth we live in a kind of **greenhouse**. During the daytime sunlight shines through the atmosphere and warms Earth's surface. At night Earth's surface cools. Heat from its surface is released back into the air. Some of the heat is trapped by gases in the atmosphere. This is called the **greenhouse effect**. The **greenhouse gases** work like the glass walls and roof of a greenhouse that keep heat inside.

Greenhouse gases are important because they keep Earth warm. Do you enjoy the warmth you feel on a summer day? You can thank the gases! They also help plants and trees grow on our planet. But we have to make sure we don't produce too many greenhouse gases, or Earth will be in trouble. Make your own greenhouse to explore Earth's heating and cooling!

What You Do

1. Before you begin, use a pencil and your notebook to draw a table with the information shown.

What You Need

pencil and notebook

2 glass thermometers

clear glass bowl, large enough to cover one of the thermometers

plastic wrap

watch or timer

Time (minutes)	Temperature in Grass	Temperature in Bowl
Start		
5		
10		
15		
20		
25		
30		

greenhouse—a warm building where plants can grow

greenhouse effect—the trapping of heat by a thick atmosphere or glass

greenhouse gases—gases in a planet's atmosphere that trap heat energy from the sun

What You Do, continued

2. Go to a backyard or park. Place one **thermometer** on the grass. Place the other thermometer inside a clear glass bowl. Cover the bowl with plastic wrap. The thermometers should be in direct sunlight and near each other.

Helpful Hint: Make sure there are no shadows over the thermometers.

3. Take a reading from each thermometer. Write down the temperatures measured in the "Start" row. Do not remove the plastic wrap from the bowl; try to read the temperature through the plastic.

4. Using a watch or timer, take readings from each thermometer every five minutes, for 30 minutes. Enter your results in your notebook.

Which thermometer warmed up the quickest? Can you think of reasons why the temperatures might be different?

TRY THIS:

Repeat the experiment on different surfaces, such as a sidewalk, sandy beach, bare soil, or in the shade. Leave the thermometers out overnight and measure the temperatures first thing in the morning—and then monitor them throughout the day.

Greenhouse gases keep Earth warm—and that's a good thing! But scientists have shown that burning **fossil fuels** and other human activities have caused a lot of greenhouse gases to be released into the atmosphere. These extra greenhouse gases cause **global warming**. Warmer temperatures can be dangerous for polar bears, for example, if their icy homes melt.

Want to help prevent global warming? Remember to reduce, reuse, and recycle! Reducing the amount of stuff you buy reduces the amount of waste you have. You can also turn off lights when you're not using them. Reuse whatever you can, such as plastic bags, instead of throwing them away. You can also donate clothes and toys that you don't use anymore. If you can't reuse something, recycle it! Common items to recycle are plastic milk or juice jugs, aluminum cans, and newspapers.

thermometer–a tool that measures temperature

fossil fuel–**a** natural fuel formed from the remains of plants and animals; coal, oil, and natural gas are fossil fuels

global warming–a steady rise in the temperature of Earth's atmosphere

17

Water Makes the World Go 'Round

Rain or shine, water is constantly **evaporating** from oceans, lakes, and streams all over the world. Water **condenses** in clouds and later returns to Earth as rain or snow.

This process is called the water cycle. On a sunny day, try making a miniature version of Earth's water cycle with a **solar still!**

evaporate–to change from a liquid to a vapor or a gas

condense–to change from a gas to a liquid

solar still–a device that uses the sun to distill salt to produce drinkable water

What You Do

What You Need

- small drinking glass
- bowl large enough to hold the glass
- drinking water (tap or bottled)
- measuring spoons
- salt
- wooden spoon
- plastic wrap
- rubber band
- small weight, such as a rock

1. Wash the glass and bowl to make sure they are clean enough to drink from.

2. Put the glass inside the bowl and pour drinking water into the bowl. Make sure the water is slightly lower than the top of the glass.

3. Remove the glass and add 1 teaspoon (5 grams) salt to the water. Stir with a wooden spoon until the salt dissolves. It's OK if a few grains of salt remain at the bottom of the bowl.

4. Put the glass back into the bowl. Cover the bowl and glass with plastic wrap, securing with a rubber band.

5. Place a small rock or some other weight on top of the plastic wrap. The weight should cause the wrap to stretch a bit lower just above the glass.

6. Carefully place the bowl outside in the sun. Leave it outside for a few hours.

7. Taste the water that collected in the glass. It should taste fresh and not salty.

What happened to the salt? How is your solar still like the water cycle?

Earth's Systems

Earth is made up of four major systems called spheres. All of the rocks, minerals, and dirt, both on Earth's surface and deep below, make up the geosphere. The hydrosphere is made up of all of the water on Earth, including rivers, lakes, and oceans, frozen ice caps and glaciers, and moisture in the air. The atmosphere is a layer of gases surrounding Earth, like a big blanket. And you are part of the biosphere—all of Earth's living things, from fleas to whales.

You Can Be a Microbe Farmer

The soil under your feet and in your backyard or park is part of the geosphere. It's also home to many living things, including an amazing number of **microbes**. Soil microbes constantly reuse and recycle nutrients and chemicals in the soil including sulfur, oxygen, and carbon.

Like other living things, microbes need certain environments in which to live. You can make your own microbe farm to see the amazing things living in the dirt!

microbe—a tiny living thing that is too small to be seen without a microscope

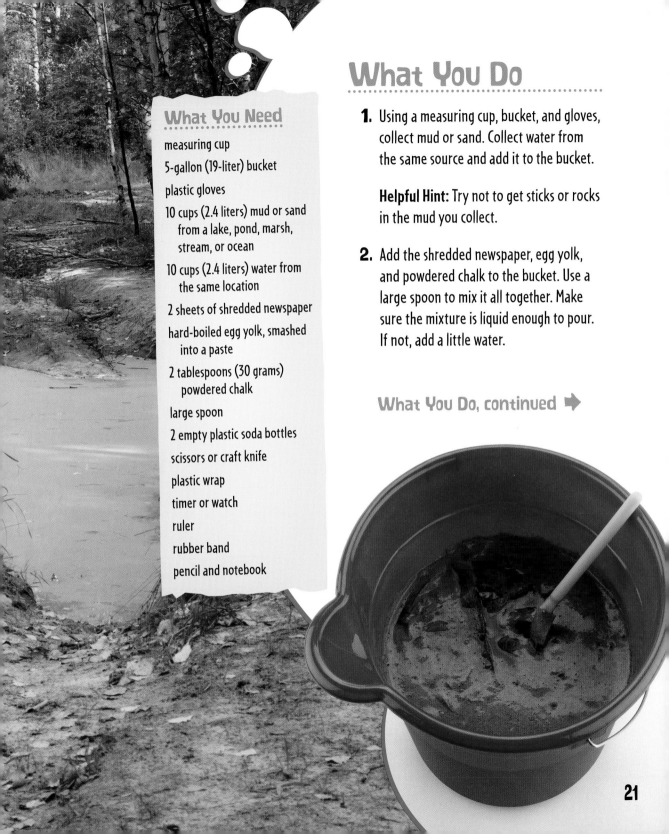

What You Need

measuring cup

5-gallon (19-liter) bucket

plastic gloves

10 cups (2.4 liters) mud or sand
   from a lake, pond, marsh,
   stream, or ocean

10 cups (2.4 liters) water from
   the same location

2 sheets of shredded newspaper

hard-boiled egg yolk, smashed
   into a paste

2 tablespoons (30 grams)
   powdered chalk

large spoon

2 empty plastic soda bottles

scissors or craft knife

plastic wrap

timer or watch

ruler

rubber band

pencil and notebook

What You Do

1. Using a measuring cup, bucket, and gloves, collect mud or sand. Collect water from the same source and add it to the bucket.

   Helpful Hint: Try not to get sticks or rocks in the mud you collect.

2. Add the shredded newspaper, egg yolk, and powdered chalk to the bucket. Use a large spoon to mix it all together. Make sure the mixture is liquid enough to pour. If not, add a little water.

What You Do, continued ➡

3. Wash the plastic bottles and remove the labels. Ask an adult to help you cut the tops off the bottles to use as funnels.

4. Using the bottle top funnels, carefully pour a small amount of the mud mixture into each bottle. Place your hand over the top of the bottle and tap the bottom of the bottle on the table.

5. Repeat step 4 several times, until each bottle is nearly full. Stir the mixture to remove any air bubbles.

6. Let the bottles sit for about 30 minutes. You should have about ½ inch (2 centimeters) of water on top of the mud mixture. Remove excess water if needed.

7. Cover the bottles with plastic wrap and secure with a rubber band.

8. Place one of the bottles in a dark room or under a box. Place the other bottle in a sunny room but not in direct sunlight.

9. Draw a picture of the bottles and record your observations. Now comes the hard part: wait!

10. In one week, repeat step 9. Repeat step 9 for six to eight weeks.

Compare the bottles in the sunny and dark rooms. Various microbes, like other living things, need special conditions to live and grow. The microbes that live near the top, middle, and bottom of your microbe farm all have different growing conditions. What did you observe in each bottle? Did your observations change as the weeks went by?

FACT

There are more microbes in a teaspoon of soil than there are people on Earth! They are necessary to plants and other living things that grow in the soil.

Fun with Gravity

Mercury

Venus

Earth

Mars

Jupiter

Uranus

Saturn

Neptune

24

Earth is one of eight planets that **orbit** the sun, which makes it our very own star! Planets and other objects orbit the sun for the very same reason a dropped ball falls to the ground—gravity.

Gravity is the force of attraction between two objects with mass. Bigger objects produce a larger gravitational pull than smaller ones, and the sun is the biggest object in the solar system. The sun pulls the planets toward it while they are in orbit. Now you can explore gravity in an experiment made famous hundreds of years ago!

orbit—to travel around an object in space

What You Do

1. Draw a table in your notebook with the information shown.

What You Need

pencil and notebook

helper, such as a friend or an adult

ladder or step stool

two balls of approximately the same size but different mass, such as a ping-pong ball and a golf ball, or a tennis ball and a baseball

two sheets of paper

Trial #	Heavy ball	Light ball	Same time
1			
2			
3			
4			
5			
6			
7			
8			
9			
10			
Total			

2. Have a helper stand in front of the ladder or step stool. Your helper can retrieve the objects you drop and hand them back to you as you go through the experiment.

3. Climb the ladder or step stool with the two similar-sized balls.

4. Drop the two balls from the same height at the same time. It can be tricky to drop the two balls at exactly the same time and height, so try it a few times.

5. Record your results in the data table in your notebook, putting a check in the box of which ball landed first. If the balls land at the same time, put a check in the "Same time" column.

6. Draw another data table in your notebook. Repeat the experiment with pieces of paper. Crumple one sheet into a ball, and leave the other piece flat. Drop the two objects from the same height at the same time. Try crumpling up the second sheet of paper and repeat.

With the balls, did one of them hit the ground first, or did they land at the same time? Did the crumpled sheet of paper behave differently from the flat sheet? Can you explain your results?

Galileo

In the late 1500s, most people thought that heavier objects would fall faster than lighter ones. An Italian scientist named Galileo Galilei decided to settle the question once and for all. Legend has it that he climbed to the top of a tall tower in Pisa and dropped two balls of different masses to test his theory that they would fall at the same rate. Galileo found that all objects fall at the same rate, regardless of their mass.

A Sunny Clock

Imagine standing on a sidewalk as the sun rises in the morning. Where is your shadow? As the day goes on, your shadow would most likely change and move as the sun moves. When the sun sets and it's dark out, you wouldn't have a shadow anymore.

Before clocks were invented, people used the movement of the sun to tell time. Are you ready to tell time based on the sun's movement? Give it a shot, and make your own **sundial**!

sundial—an instrument that shows the time by using sunlight; a pointer casts a shadow that moves slowly around a flat, marked dial

What You Do

What You Need

ruler

paper plate with slightly curved up sides

sharp pencil

markers

plastic straw

4 nails

watch or timer

1. Use a ruler to find the exact center of the paper plate and mark it with a pencil. Use the pencil to poke a hole through the center point.

2. If you wish to begin at 7:00 a.m. write the number 7 on one edge of the plate with a marker.

Helpful Hint: The time you choose to begin will be determined by the time of year and day length. The activity takes a day to complete, so pick a day when you have no school or other activities.

3. At 7:00 a.m. on a sunny day, take the plate and straw outside. Put the plate on the ground in a spot where it will stay sunny.

4. Poke the straw through the center hole. Turn the plate so the shadow of the straw points to the number 7.

5. Fasten the plate to the ground with the nails.

6. Check the plate exactly one hour later, at 8 a.m. Use a marker to label the position of the shadow on the edge of the plate and write the number 8 on that spot. Continue doing this throughout the day until sundown. You should have a completed sundial!

Life on Earth

We have seasons because of Earth's motion as it orbits the sun. Without the sun, there would be no life on Earth. Other things make life on Earth possible, as well, such as weather, water, and gravity. These dynamic systems on our planet are all around you—all you have to do is look!

29

Glossary

anemometer (a-nuh-MOM-uh-tuhr)—a scientific instrument used to measure wind speed

climate (KLY-muht)—the usual weather that occurs in a place

condense (kuhn-DENS)—to change from a gas to a liquid

convection (kuhn-VEK-shuhn)—the movement of heat through liquids and gases

density (DEN-si-tee)—relationship of an object's mass to its volume

energy (E-nuhr-jee)—the ability to do work, such as moving things or giving heat or light

equator (i-KWAY-tuhr)—an imaginary line around the middle of Earth; it divides the northern and southern hemispheres

evaporate (i-VA-puh-rayt)— to change from a liquid to a vapor or a gas

fossil fuel (FAH-suhl FYOOL)—a natural fuel formed from the remains of plants and animals; coal, oil, and natural gas are fossil fuels

global warming (GLOH-buhl WORM-ing)— a steady rise in the temperature of Earth's atmosphere

greenhouse (GREEN-houss)—a warm building where plants can grow

greenhouse effect (GREEN-houss uh-FEKT)—the trapping of heat by a thick atmosphere or glass

greenhouse gases (GREEN-houss GASS-iz)—gases in a planet's atmosphere that trap heat energy from the sun

high pressure (HYE PRESH-ur)—a condition of the atmosphere in which the pressure is above average

low pressure (LOH PRESH-ur)—a condition of the atmosphere in which the pressure is below average

microbe (MYE-krobe)—a tiny living thing that is too small to be seen without a microscope

orbit (OR-bit)—to travel around an object in space

solar still (SOH-lur STIL)—a device that uses the sun to distill salt to produce drinkable water

sundial (SUHN-dye-uhl)—an instrument that shows the time by using sunlight; a pointer casts a shadow that moves slowly around a flat, marked dial

temperature (TEM-pur-uh-chur)—the measure of how hot or cold something is; room temperature is typically a comfortable 70 degrees Fahrenheit (21 degrees Celsius)

thermometer (thur-MOM-uh-tur)—a tool that measures temperature

Read More

Hunter, Nick. *Earth.* Astronaut Travel Guides. Chicago: Raintree, 2013.

Taylor-Butler, Christine. *The Sun.* A True Book. New York: Children's Press, 2014.

Thomas, Isabel. *Experiments with Heating and Cooling.* Read and Experiment. Chicago: Capstone Raintree, 2015.

Internet Sites

FactHound offers a safe, fun way to find Internet sites related to this book. All of the sites on FactHound have been researched by our staff.

Here's all you do:
Visit *www.facthound.com*
Type in this code: **9781491448144**

Check out projects, games and lots more at
www.capstonekids.com

Index